A Hippopotamus Grows Up

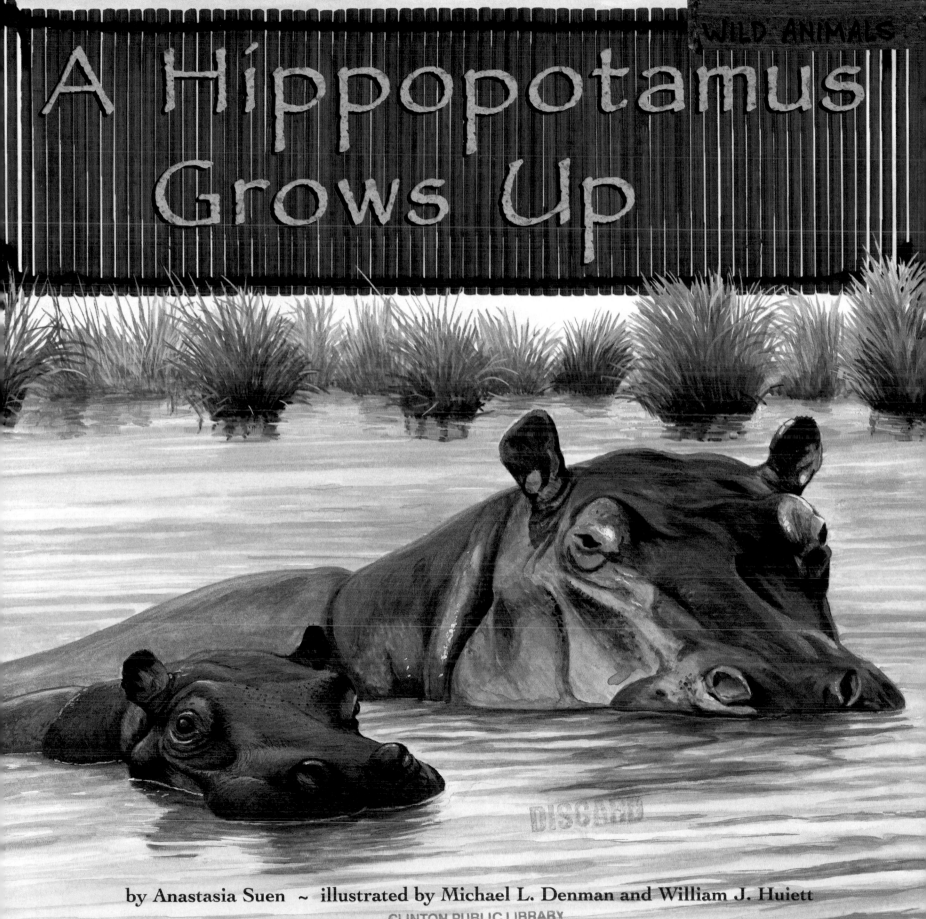

by Anastasia Suen ~ illustrated by Michael L. Denman and William J. Huiett

Thanks to our advisers for their expertise, research, and advice:

Michelle Stancer, Keeper
Zoological Society of San Diego
San Diego Zoo
San Diego, California

Susan Kesselring, M.A., Literacy Educator
Rosemount–Apple Valley–Eagan (Minnesota) School District

Editorial Director: Carol Jones
Managing Editor: Catherine Neitge
Creative Director: Keith Griffin
Editor: Christianne Jones
Story Consultant: Terry Flaherty
Designer: Nathan Gassman
Production Artist: Angela Kilmer
Page Production: Picture Window Books
The illustrations in this book were created with acrylics.

Picture Window Books
5115 Excelsior Boulevard, Suite 232
Minneapolis, MN 55416
877-845-8392
www.picturewindowbooks.com

Printed in the United States of America.

Library of Congress Cataloging-in-Publication Data
Suen, Anastasia.
A hippopotamus grows up / by Anastasia Suen ; illustrated by Michael Denman and
William J. Huiett.
p. cm. — (Wild animals)
Includes bibliographical references and index.
ISBN 1-4048-0988-0 (hardcover)
1. Hippopotamidae—Infancy—Juvenile literature. 2. Hippopotamidae—Development—
Juvenile literature. I. Denman, Michael L., ill. II. Huiett, William J., 1943- ill. III. Title.
QL737.U57S77 2005
599.63'5139—dc22
                                        2005004279

Welcome to the world of wild animals! Follow a baby hippo from water to land. The calf spends most of his day in the water or rolling in the mud to cool down. Watch the hippo grow up and start a family of his own.

Under the water, a baby hippo is born. He pushes off the water's bottom and pops above the water. He takes his first breath of air.

Baby hippos are also born on land. Hippos can walk or run just minutes after they are born.

Peek-a-boo! The hippo's nose, eyes, and ears stick out of the water. The hippo can only breathe above water.

The baby hippo goes back under the water to feed. His nose and eyes close as he drinks his mother's milk.

Hippos spend at least 18 hours a day in the water. They stay in the water for so long because their skin dries out quickly in the heat.

After several weeks alone together, his
mother takes him to meet the herd.

Female hippos are called cows.
Male hippos are called bulls.
Baby hippos are called calves.

Other hippos come to greet him. Mother hippos from the herd watch the baby hippo when his mother goes off to eat.

Time to eat! At four months, the calf can eat grass. As the sun goes down, the calf follows his mother to her eating place.

After calves stop drinking milk, they only eat plants. They follow their mothers on private eating trails.

After they eat, the calf and his mother go back into the water.

Splash! In the cool water, the calf plays with other male calves. They learn to fight through "play fighting."

Growl! Snort! Roar! The calves make a lot of noises as they play. They open their mouths wide to show their teeth.

Hippos have tusks like elephants, but a hippo's tusks are inside its mouth.

The calf spends most of his day in the water. Now he is big enough to walk on the bottom of the lake.

Adult hippos can stay under water for five to six minutes. They are too heavy to float or swim, so they walk on the bottom instead.

The calf takes a deep breath and sinks
under. When he goes under water, fish
nibble on him and clean his skin.

Hot, hot, hot! Out of the water, the sun burns the young hippo's skin. He rolls in the mud to cool down.

When the mud on his back dries, the calf goes back to the water. An egret lands on his back and eats bugs off his skin.

When a hippo stays in the sun too long, it sweats a red goo that looks like blood.

As the young bull grows, he plays with the older bulls.

When the young bull reaches maturity, he leaves the herd. He finds a partner and mates.

A bull's territory is called a refuge.

A new hippo is born. The young bull is now a father. The mother brings the new calf to meet the herd. The new calf will grow up on the African plains, just like her parents.

Hippos are one of the largest animals living on land.

① **SKIN** Hippos have gray-blue skin. However, their sweat is thick, oily, and pinkish-red in color.

② **NOSTRILS** A hippo can close its nostrils when it goes under the water.

③ **MOUTH** Before a hippo fights, it yawns to show its teeth. Its giant mouth can open 4 feet (1.2 meters) wide.

④ **LEGS** Even with short, stumpy legs, hippos can run 18 miles (28.8 kilometers) an hour.

Map

There are two types of hippos—the common hippo and the Pygmy hippo. The hippos in this book are common hippos. Both types of hippos live in Africa.

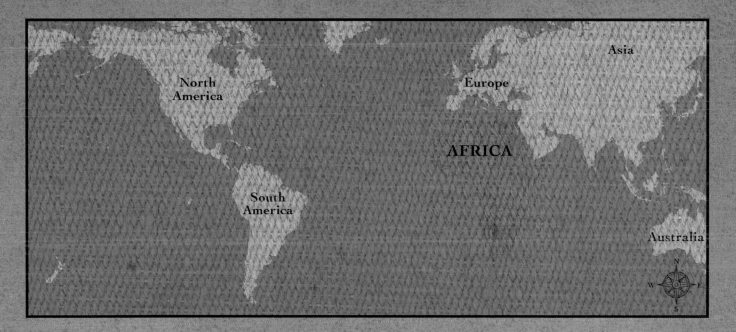

Glossary

bull—an adult male hippo
calf—a young hippo
cow—an adult female hippo
egret—a wading bird with long legs
herd—a group of animals that live together
refuge—the territory of an adult male hippo
territory—the place an animal claims as its own
tusks—long, ivory teeth

To Learn More

At the Library

Cole, Melissa. *Hippos.* San Diego: Blackbirch Press, 2002.
Kendall, Patricia. *Hippos.* Chicago: Raintree, 2004.
Stewart, Melissa. *Hippopotomuses.* New York: Children's Press, 2002.

On the Web

FactHound offers a safe, fun way to find Web sites related to this book. All of the sites on FactHound have been researched by our staff. *www.facthound.com*

1. Visit the FactHound home page.

2. Enter a search word related to this book, or type in this special code: 1404809880

3. Click on the FETCH IT button.

Your trusty FactHound will fetch the best sites for you!

Index

Look for all of the books in the Wild Animals series:

A Baboon Grows Up   A Rhinoceros Grows Up
A Hippopotamus Grows Up   A Tiger Grows Up
A Lion Grows Up   An Elephant Grows Up